During one week in 1998, 80 percent of the coral reefs around the world suffered coral bleaching. Many have since recovered, but 40 percent of all reefs remain in jeopardy. • Another threat to reefs is ocean acidification. The ocean absorbs 25 percent of the earth's carbon dioxide (CO_2), so the chemicals released into the air also end up in the sea. When carbon emissions from cars and factories dissolve in the water, they create an acid that causes shells and coral reefs to dissolve.

Ocean Commotion

Ocean Commotion

LIFE ON THE REEF

By Janeen Mason

PELICAN PUBLISHING COMPANY

GRETNA 2010

For Kaila—Love, Nee Nee

This book is made possible by the love and support of Kevin and Penny—thank you both from the bottom of my reef-roving soul—and by scientists the world over who give their time and intellect to the spectacular world beneath our ocean's surface.

In memory of Mae Slaton

*The word "Pelican" and the depiction of a pelican
are trademarks of Pelican Publishing Company, Inc.,
and are registered in the U.S. Patent and Trademark Office.*

Library of Congress Cataloging-in-Publication Data

Mason, Janeen I.
  Ocean commotion : life on the reef / Janeen Mason.
    p. cm.
  ISBN 978-1-58980-783-9 (hardcover : alk. paper) 1. Hermit crabs 2. Coral reef animals—Juvenile literature. 3. Molting—Juvenile literature. 4. Coral reef ecology—Juvenile literature. I. Title.
  QL444.M33M37 2010
  578.77'89—dc22

                         2010012933

Printed in Singapore
Published by Pelican Publishing Company, Inc.
1000 Burmaster Street, Gretna, Louisiana 70053

OCEAN COMMOTION: LIFE ON THE REEF

Under warm, rolling waves on a clear blue Florida dawn, the first rays of sunlight danced across the reef. A **hermit crab** squeezed and squished her soft belly into a tulip shell. *Oops!* She wouldn't fit.

A nosy **pufferfish** unexpectedly ballooned when the crab tumbled out into the open.

During each **molt** the crab grew. Her **carapace,** or hard outer skin, split open and her body emerged from the old skin. She looked the same, only bigger. Her bright new body armor started out soft so when she molted, she had to hide long enough for it to harden.

Her belly stayed spongy, so she kept it tucked safely inside a borrowed shell she carried everywhere. Normally she could vanish inside it to hide, but not this morning. She had practically doubled in size overnight. She needed to find a new shell—today.

She tapped her claws together, lifted her too-small tulip shell, tiptoed through a garden of **anemones,** and waved to a family of **cleaner shrimp** nearby.

They froze. It took them a minute to recognize her. The biggest one waved back and parachuted into the mouth of a **grouper** docked below. They all bowed in her direction and went back to work plucking **parasites** for breakfast.

Crunch. Crunch. Crunch. A **school** of **parrotfish** munched across the coral head. She rolled just as one nipped the tip of her shell.

The hermit crab crawled up onto a ledge to get a better view. Sunlight sparkled on an empty jar wedged between the sponges. *Eureka!*

She darted across the open, pried her back end free from her tight shell, and slipped it into the jar. It felt cool and smooth inside, and she could look out through the glass. But she didn't see the grumpy **decorator crab.**

She lost her balance and tumbled over the edge of the reef. She bounced down and down. She grabbed for anything to stop herself, but with a *clink* and a *chink,* she crashed against an abandoned boat anchor. Her jar cracked.

The crab spent the rest of the day limping across the grass flats where **conch** shells lay **camouflaged** by **turtle grass.**

Tap. Tap. Tap. Each one was occupied.

The water grew darker and the sound of thunder rumbled through the sea. She finally found an empty shell. She lugged and pulled and heaved it over onto its back. A cloud of sand billowed out.

Lightning exploded above, and the hermit crab hurtled from the broken jar into the heavy conch. A powerful wave pounded the flats and swept it off the bottom. Roiling water washed her in and out of the shell, but she clung to its lip with all her might. The wave weakened and the shell dropped. *Clunk.*

As the storm raged, night fell.

She awoke from her exhausted dreams and peeked out. **Sea stars** blinked, **jellyfish** shimmered, and tiny **copepods** trailed delicate streams of light. It was a dazzling show of **bioluminescence.**

In the morning she discovered that she had landed on bleached and broken coral littering a barren reef. All her hair stood on end. **Sea urchins** marched into the dark crevasses in single file. Vacant shells lay everywhere.

Leaving behind the heavy conch shell, she skittered across the rubble with her soft belly exposed. Her claws shook as she hurried to try on one shell after another. *Too big* . . . *Too small* . . . And then . . .

The whelk shell felt smooth and cool inside. Not too heavy, not too light. She lifted it up, set it down, wiggled it around.

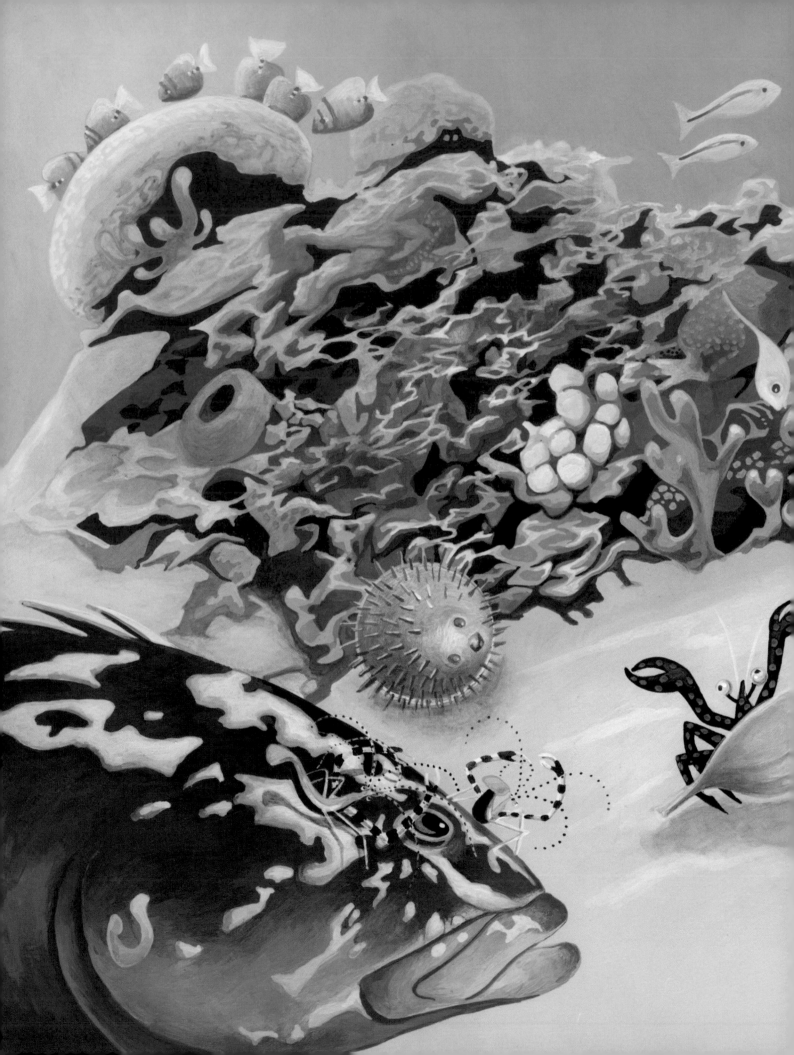

Click. Click. Click. Her **antennae** quivered, and the hermit crab turned to follow the sound of a school of **surgeonfish** she recognized on their morning rounds. She tapped her claws together and danced across the bottom, all the way toward home.

Illustrated Glossary

anemone: a soft saltwater animal that looks like a flower attached to the ocean floor. It has a mouth and tentacles, but no skeleton.

antennae: threadlike structures on the heads of animals such as crabs that are used to smell, touch, sense vibration and sound, and even taste.

bioluminescence: the production of light from within by some living creatures.

camouflaged: disguised to look like an animal or plant's surroundings.

carapace: hard outer skin that protects the soft bodies of crustaceans.

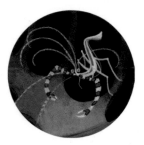

cleaner shrimp: brightly colored shrimp that feed on parasites living on larger fish.

conch: a large saltwater mollusk, similar to a snail, with a spiral shell.

copepods: a group of tiny crustaceans with long bodies that light up at night to attract a mate or scare off creatures that might harm them.

crustacean: an underwater creature with a hard shell or crust instead of skin.

decorator crab: a crab that camouflages itself by attaching anemones, small corals, and other found objects to its shell.

grouper: a family of large fish that lives in warm waters.

hermit crab: a crab that protects its soft belly by occupying an abandoned shell.

jellyfish: a soft sea creature with a dome and tentacles that drifts in the current. It has no eyes, no heart, and no brain.

molt: the process of shedding and replacing the outer covering of skin.

parasite: an animal or plant that lives on another creature, getting its food from the body of its host. Parasites can be painful, even dangerous to its animal host.

parrotfish: brightly colored fish with parrot-like beaks that munch on coral and excrete sand.

pufferfish: a type of fish that fills itself with water or air to appear larger when threatened.

sea stars: also known as starfish, many of these animals can produce their own light. They have the ability to regrow missing limbs.

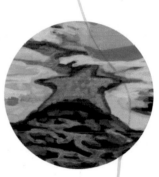

school: a large group of fish living and feeding together.

sea urchin: a sphere-shaped animal protected by hard spines.

surgeonfish: a fish with sharp fins near the tail.

turtle grass: sea grass that grows near the coastlines where it provides food and homes for many creatures.

Dear Reader,

I am writing this letter to you while sitting next to the ocean that I love. The wind is gentle on my face and the sound of waves in the background mingles with the voices of children playing in the surf. At this beach, many years ago, I put on a mask and snorkel and looked underwater for the first time. It changed the direction of my life. I knew then that someday I would write and illustrate this book.

My children grew up on this beach. It is where they learned to swim and dive and where they scouted for nesting sea turtles on warm summer nights. Now my grandchildren spend bright, sunny days here. We have seen everything from hermit crabs like the one in this story to schools of spinner sharks. I am so grateful to be able to share my passion with them, and with you.

I hope you are inspired to learn more about coral reefs and the animals that depend on them to thrive. In my lifetime I have witnessed our delicate reefs struggle to survive coral bleaching events (like the one in the lonely spot where our hermit crab in the story found her new shell). But recently scientists have identified a new complication called ocean acidification. The chemical composition of the ocean is changing. This is brought about by carbon emissions from cars, factories, and power plants around the world. Whatever we put in our atmosphere ends up in our ocean. Ocean acidification causes shells to soften and dissolve. This could mean the end of pteropods (sea butterflies) and copepods, of crab and shrimp and lobster, and of our precious coral reefs. This will affect the entire food chain.

It is going to be up to your generation to develop clean power and share your technology with the world. Your discoveries will save the planet. Although we may never meet in person, my grandchildren's grandchildren, and yours too, may one day benefit from us meeting here in the pages of this book. Across time and distance, I thank you.

Sincerely,

"If we were logical the future would be bleak indeed. But we are more than logical. We are human beings, and we have faith, and we have hope, and we can work."
—Jacques Yves Cousteau

Coral reefs are endangered worldwide, and their destruction is occurring much faster than scientists anticipated. Children all over the globe are engaging in programs to save the reefs. Contact the following organizations online for information on what you can do to make a difference:

CoralWatch, University of Queensland, Australia

Ocean Research and Conservation Association

National Atmospheric and Oceanographic Administration Coral Reef Conservation Program

Reef Relief Environmental Center